Mosaic

Natalie Pockett

For Mr Robinson, who first showed me
what poetry could look like and
helped me believe that I could write it.

Contents

Green

They fill the houses' garden beds	1
Prairie farmers' fields	3
Sunsets over waters	4
A moment	5
Fields of bright, yellow dandelions	6
Grass river	8
Animals	9
Flowers	11

Pink

Grocery store succulent	15
I still look for you	16
Great romance	17
Fuck you	18
His family	19
Something new	20
The second time around	21
You make my blood bubble	23
Ruin me	24
Family matters	26
Hurt	27
Long-distance cousins	28
Slipping away	29
Bridesmaids	30
Hey! How are you?	31
Our thirsty houseplant	32
Drinks	33

Grey

Homesick	37
Imaginary me	38
Loneliness	39
Ghost	40
Glasses	41
That's what did it!	42
I'm afraid of heights	43
Seat A8	44
Mind reader	45
I'm feeling depressed right now	46
Balance	48
Run out of words	49
Untitled	40

Red

Pop!	53
The blue door	55
Panic	56
News	58
Love your neighbour	60
Mosaic	62
Somewhere in this world	63
I dress like this	65
Civilized	66
Get your shit together	67
Birthday wishes	69

Green

*If you truly love nature,
you will find beauty everywhere.*

– Vincent Van Gogh

They fill the houses' garden beds

Bushes of pale pink peonies
bloom one at a time.
Unborn flowers sway
covered by ants as they climb.

Irises stretch up higher and higher,
they line worn, wooden fences
with their multi-purple petals.
They signal us as good weather commences.

Tall, tall sunflowers
see over the roofs.
They try to reach the sky
before their petals start to droop.

Fuschia hang upside down,
pointing their petals to the ground.
In every colour they look below,
to the green, green stems to which they're bound

Simple daisies flood the yard,
more emerge each year as they spread.
Their snow white petals catch the eye
and a sweet scent they keep embedded.

The first flower friends to see the sun,
red and pink tulips are already gone,
but the joy they spark is not yet lost,
their crumbled leaves feed the flowers now across the lawn.

Prairie farmers' fields

Fields of who-knows-what
stretch as far as the eye can see.
For as far as I can see,
prairie farmers' fields grow
plush as floating clouds.
Let me lay down my head
on the prairie farmers' fields
of soft who-knows-what.
They sway in the wind
to rock me to sleep.
They grow softly to be
a green prairie mattress
just for me.

Sunsets over waters

Every sunset is
a new work of art
brushed across
the delicate canvas
that separates us
from the moon and the stars,
and that draws a line
between waters and colours.

A moment

For a moment you're sitting on top of a picnic table at the edge of a different world.

Soft winds cancel out the burn of a summer sun
and ripple the water in a way that seems
too perfectly fragmented and beautiful to be real.
The sky is bright-bright blue,
a soft rainbow palate starts to take over.
The indigo clouds glide so slowly across the sky
that they almost aren't moving at all.
The only thing between you and the other world
is a line of rough boulders
and a butter-smooth beach.
All of a sudden a flock of birds
bloom from the treetops
and flee into the bright-bright blue sky.

For a moment you're sitting here in a picture perfect frame of life — the moment becomes a memory that could restart a hollow and broken heart.

Fields of bright, yellow dandelions

and the strange way that they don't grow in the place of a future desire path.

The crushed, red berries that litter the sidewalk under their mother tree.

Pink tulips that have only just bloomed, months before their neighbours.

A big bumble bee bobbing clumsily between flowers.

The soft heat of the sun as it shines through patches of clouds.

Puddles of cool water that seeps through the toes of shoes.

Vibrate, green grass that reaches out from the ground to tickle any ankle it can.

The slight chill on skin that is bare for the first time in months.

Another bird that's come back to sing from its new home up high.

The laughter of children who are once again free to roll in the grass.

The rustle of fresh green leaves in the warm, spring breeze.

Blooming lilacs of white and purple that flood the streets with their sweet, sweet fragrance.

Grass and dirt, just after a sun shower.

Fruit that has finally started to taste like it should again.

Grass river

There's a river of grass
growing up through a crack
in the worn sidewalk.
As the year goes,
the grass ebbs and it grows
and paints a broken thing
bright green.

Animals

The trust that animals have in us
to keep them safe and fed
is astonishing.

That the cat I just met
feels safe asleep in my lap,
that she asks me for love
and belly scratches.

That my dogs drink their water
when we aren't at home.
They know that someone
will come back.

That the pigeon sits
on the bus station divider,
watching us all watch him
knowing he's safe from the bus.

And that the dog being walked
by its man down the street
walks straight up to me
to pet its ears with no fear
of pain or danger.

Wouldn't it be nice
if people could trust people
to just care
for each other?

But people only care
for the things they like
and people don't really seem to like
each other.

Flowers

Brightly coloured
and sweet smelling.

Does that not describe
a dandelion?

Why are they sprayed
with chemicals,

while other flowers sit
revered in glass homes.

Pink

*I thought, briefly, that I would never feel
as intensely connected to the world, to another
human being, as I did at that moment.*

– Jojo Moyes' *Me Before You*

Grocery store succulent

So lonely that I feel it
in my blood
and my lungs
and the beating of my heart.
But I don't know how to text
so I get a plant
from the grocery store.
Resilient little things,
they can outlast almost any relationship.
Not that I have one anymore.

I still look for you

In the places we used to go,
and the bus lines you sometimes ride,
and any place you've ever mentioned.
I'm not sure what I'd do if I found you.
Would I duck behind a shelf,
or make small talk
like I didn't know everything about you.

I've started looking for you
in everyone I meet,
any hint of similarity fills me
with dread.
Will he fool me into loving him too?
I wonder if I'll ever stop looking for you,
or if you will forever be a ghost
that haunts the faces of everyone else.

Great romance

I want my own great romance
like the ones that line my shelves
and fill my daydreams.
I want to be swept off my feet,
I want to be cherished,
I want to be worshiped.
I want more
than anyone in my world
can give me.

Fuck you

Cause now I panic
at the slightest
uncomfortable feeling.
You've got me thinking
you all want to hurt me the same.
I can't have a normal
relationship
cause I'm looking
for anything
I can think
is wrong.

His family

I hope I didn't disappoint his family
when I left.
It's just too bad I met them
very much too fast.
We should have planned to wait
until later on so that
the only ones I hurt
would have been me and him.

Something new

I had forgotten how happy I can be
at a good morning text,
and how excited I could be
to see someone on a Thursday afternoon.
The grey clouds of self loathing and anger
turned all relationships dark in my mind,
that is until I met you.

The second time around

It's somehow easier
but harder all at once.
I know how it feels to be
broken hearted
but also how good it is to be
in love.

The second time around
I'm not worried about myself.
I know now that
I can be loved
and I can be wanted
just not if he's the one
to do that.

The second time around
I'm more afraid of butterflies.
I know how fast
something can change
from good to bad.

But the second time around
is so much better
than the first.
This time I'm not
lying about how I feel
because I know what is love
and what definitely is not.

So this time around
when he kisses me
in the front seat
I know I don't feel love
but it's still better
than what I felt at the end
of the first time around.

You make my blood bubble

like there's champagne
running through my veins
and my head dizzy.
But the good dizzy,
like riding a rollercoaster
not like falling down the stairs.
You've awoken the butterflies
that had been resting
in my stomach.
Now their fluttering wings
signal happiness
rather than the usual dread.
You make my eyes sparkle
with every smile
that you pull from my lips.
If I had a pay-per phone plan
I'd be deeply in debt
because all I want to do
when I'm not with you
is hear your voice
and read your words.
All I want to do
when I am with you
is bask in the electric feeling
of love
that you've infected me with.

Ruin me

Right now
I think
you might
make me
run out
of things
to write
poems about.
They don't
come out
as well
when I'm
feeling happy.

Or maybe you will
ruin me so thoroughly
that my words will
flow for the rest
of my life, I'll
write the kinds of
poems that no one
wants to read about
themselves. You could shatter
my heart into a
thousand tiny fragments, and
each would spell out
a new line of
devestation and of regret.

I'm not quite sure
which is more terrifying.
For joy
to make
me lose
my words,
or for sadness to
dictate all my poems.

Family matters

Every second of every day
I get to feel villainized
for loving my whole family.
A nightmare I'll never wake up from.

I hope that no one hates me
for loving the people they don't
but if my biggest crime in life is
loving,
I think I'll have done alright.

It's a special kind of lonely,
because there's not a single person
that I can tell.
Not without sparking that feeling of guilt
or sharing family matters
to someone without family ties.

Hurt

It's a special kind of hurt
learning that someone you love
hurt someone you love.
A swirling mess of
confusion and confliction,
the national anthem of
children of divorce.

Long-distance cousins

I watch you grow up
through photos and videos.
Learning to ride a bike with
no training wheels,
singing 'happy birthday'
only in a video.
We share our lives in
bits and pieces,
and each time I look
you've grown even more.
Long-distance cousins,
bonded by texts,
and occasional visits,
and the eighth of our DNA
that looks the same.

Slipping away

There's something about watching someone you love
grow old,
their skin thins,
their brain dulls,
you can feel them slipping away.
Aging is the inevitable consequence
of a life well lived.
But if I have to watch
my mom
and my dad
slip away like that,
well,
I'm not quite sure that I can.

Bridesmaids

With every passing year
my future bridal party
grows emptier.
Every friend I have,
I push them away.

The pressure I feel
to find love, comes
partly from the fear
of having no one left
to hold my bouquet.

Hey! How are you?

Sorry that I haven't been in touch, you know how bad I am at this stuff. But then you haven't been in touch either, so I guess we're both to blame. How's life? How's your sister? How's the new job? With every passing day I feel myself knowing less and less about you. Isn't it crazy that we used to talk everyday? We wanted to move to a farm together and now I only see you every couple months. Isn't it crazy how fast things can change?

I wonder if your favourite colour is still purple and if you're still obsessed with Harry Styles. Do you still have all your baby names picked out and a dream wedding planned? Do you still drink the chocolate chip fraps from Starbucks? Will you still jump into the lake on September long?

I'm doing okay; I miss you like crazy but I have some really great things going for me right now. Did you know I got a cat? And that I have an almost-boyfriend? Probably not, I haven't told you after all.

I promise to text sooner next time, I think about doing it every day. I don't know what stops me. I guess I'm just scared that one of these times I'll check in to see how you're doing, and you won't text me back.

But I'm not actually going to say any of that to you. Instead I'll just say: *'Hey! How are you?'*

Our thirsty houseplant

I hope that all the people that I've hurt or left behind think about me far less than I think about them. Spare not a single thought for me, I was the one that let our relationship wither like the sad houseplant in your neighbor's window. Like them, I didn't water us. Only they forgot and I didn't; I chose to let us die of thirst.

Please, spare no thought for the girl you thought I was. She only ever existed in your head.

Drinks

I have a drink,
>　or two,
>>　　or seven,

so that I can have some fun.

I dance for an hour,
>　or two,
>>　　or four,

for the first time ever.

I talk to a stranger,
>　or two
>>　　at least,

and I don't worry about what I'm saying.

Who knew that my social issues
could be cured by a drink,
>　or two,
>>　　or seven.

Grey

*Do you ever look at someone and wonder:
what is going on inside their head?*

– Disney's *Inside Out*

Homesick

I feel homesick
for all of the lives
I wish I could be living
and all of the people
I wish I could love.

Imaginary me

There are a thousand worlds
inside my head
they swirl and grow
when I'm in bed.
And when I want to live my life
my imaginary selves invade my mind.

Loneliness

It was easier when I was more
depressed.

I could blame that for the
loneliness,

and depression can get
better.

Now that I feel
better,

I know that the loneliness is actually
my fault.

And that doesn't just get
better.

It takes work that I don't know how to do.

Ghost

I am the ghost
that haunts my home.
I lurk in dark rooms,
you can rarely catch a glimpse
of my spirit.
I am the ghost
that haunts my loves.
If you see me
run.
If I've emerged, danger comes.
I am the ghost
that haunts my dreams
with chills, doubts,
and fear.

Glasses

I wonder when I decided
glasses didn't suit my face.
Is my vision really good?
Have I just adapted to the strain?
Did I really stop needing them,
or was I lying to myself?
Did I decide they didn't suit me
before or after I was told so?
And one day,
when my eyes get too tired
to force themselves to focus,
will I get myself some glasses?
Or will I let my vision blur?

That's what did it!

Sometimes I wish I had lived through some traumatic event; like being born in a war zone or ripped from my family. That way when the darkness wins and my mind falls to pieces, I'd have something to point to. I could say: "that's what did it!" I wouldn't feel so guilty for the crazy in my head. I hate myself a little more every time I wish it.

I'm afraid of heights

Too afraid for ladders,
and diving boards,
and hot air balloons.
Too afraid for the ferris wheel,
but too embarrassed to turn away.
Up at the top the world seems
smaller,
insignificant.
In the rainbow wheel
I go up,
and my stomach stays down
along with my fear and anxiety.

Seat A8

Release day,
movie theater popcorn,
and reclining seats.
Freshly nineteen
and crying over a little
orange emotion in a
freshly thirteen
year old head.

Mind reader

I wish that I could read minds.
Not to steal information,
just so that I might be able to see
what a 'normal' brain acts like.
To compare the spiraling,
obsessive thoughts in mine
to someone else's.
I could peak into the mind
of someone truly ill
and see how I compare.
Are the ideas forced upon me
by my brain
something of concern?
Right now I am concerned
I have no way to compare
and know if the echoes
I imagine
should make me as upset
as they do.
If I could read minds I would know
if there's other people thinking this way
and I could know if they are okay
or if they are struggling
as deeply as me.

I'm feeling depressed right now

in the sense that if I could,
I would only exist in a void
with nothing but
darkness,
my mind,
and the songs that this summer has
infused into my bones.

I'm feeling depressed right now
in the sense that I want nothing more
than to be high out of my mind,
so that maybe the world could look
magical for once.

I'm feeling depressed right now
in the sense that I want to claw open
my skin and bleach my bones
to free myself
from the disgusting thoughts
and feelings
that are in me.

I'm feeling depressed right now
in the sense that I can still function
kind of
but I think if I told my therapist the truth
he might put me away
for a little while.
Maybe I should let him;
I'll probably just call in sick
and stay in bed another day.

Balance

For all the reasons that I find to
want to stay alive,
I find another reason to
want to die.
Some people are
larger than life,
but I match life's size.
Any larger,
and I run the risk
of being happy for a moment.
My life is a dangerous
balancing game
and if I'm not careful,
another drop of dread
could fall onto the plate
and could send me toppeling
off of a bridge.

Run out of words

Often I think that I've run out of words,
that there couldn't possibly be
more tales of woe in my
head.

But every time I think there's
no lines left to write,
life throws me something new
to commiserate about.

It's a miserable life when the thing
you love, requires pain
and tears
to flow on the page.

But then again,
what kind of life
is the one in which I've
run out of words.

Untitled

Watching something turn from beautiful to dangerous is a pain that goes all the way through the heart and into your lungs. Like how a field of bright yellow dandelions can so quickly become crowded with bushes of thorns. And like how childhood dreams turn into adult dread.

Red

This is the way the world ends
Not with a bang but a whimper.

– T.S. Eliot

Pop!

Life is like a balloon.
They start all small,
then start to bloom.
Multicoloured, they float
through the air.
And sometimes they

pop!

Loud and exciting
and scary all together.
They hit something sharp,
or grow far too fast,
or give into the pressure inside.

The lucky balloons never

pop!

They get to bounce
and float
and glide
until they run out of all their air.
The lucky balloons

shrivel.

Slow and quiet
and sad to watch.
Until they're back
to how they started.
Life is like a balloon,
we all get to

pop!

or

shrivel.

What would you rather do,
if you were a balloon?

The blue door

A bright blue door
on a grey, brick building
behind barbed wire
and electric fence links.
Is it a bright spot in a
bleak, grey world?
Or has its brilliance
been enveloped
by barbed wire
and electric fence links?

Panic

Cat hair on my sweater,

the soft glow of a warm white light bulb,

dusty keyboard keys and sheet music,

summer storm clouds in September,

the news titles that I try to forget about, taking residence in my searches;

my hot phone screen, bad news practically burnt into it,

candidate flyer from my mailbox that says so much but nothing,

the TV remote, can't decide whether to turn it up or off,

donation links, because the rich and powerful won't bother to care about anything;

people pleading for help, for change, for a chance at a life after this all ends,

debates about stupid, inconsequential issues that drown everything else out, grumbles of hunger in stomachs of those on every street corner;

gas where I should smell flowers,

smoke – from the fires and the bombs;

salty tears rolling past my lips,
because the panic never ends.

News

There's a new song floating around,
a little too relatable
but catchy nonetheless.

Some blonde lady is pregnant
with what must be
her hundredth blonde baby.

There's kids burning
in a car, a girl
in a ditch not far from me.

Confetti pops over our champions
in red jerseys, saying
"Viva Las Vegas!"

A prince is flying,
a king is sick,
we all joke about homeopathy.

Reddit stories layered over parkour,
"Am I the asshole?" Maybe we all are.

They are bombing tents in a refugee camp,
the place they promised was safe.

POV: Sephora 10-year-old's
get ready with me.

POV: what if it was your child?
Would anyone care then?

Teenagers raising their siblings in a tent.

When will she get a ring?

A doctor leaves cover to try and help.

People are angry about a canceled show.

Who's angry about a genocide?

Love your neighbour

"You shall not take vengeance or bear a grudge against any of your people, but you shall love your neighbour as yourself: I am the Lord." – Leviticus 19:18

Lord, I'm sorry
but I cannot love my neighbour.
If heaven is real,
save no spot for me
I cannot love my neighbour.

Not when my neighbour
is working children to death.
Not when my neighbour
is raining bombs over others.
Not when my neighbour
can watch their neighbour
die
without shedding a tear.

I cannot love a neighbour
that doesn't love
their land,
their family,
their neighbour,
their foe.
I could love a neighbour
that does not love me back,
but I cannot love a neighbour
that does not love an innocent.

I will not love my neighbour
not under these circumstances.
Not when the price is innocent lives
for my enduring soul.

Mosaic

I am a mosaic; built from the fractured pieces of all the good people that have shared this planet with me. They find me and bind themselves to every particle of my being. My humanity is the glue that allows them to stick to my soul and weigh heavily upon it.

I am a mosaic and every day I get more red.

Somewhere in this world

there's a girl,
not much younger than you.
She glides through her days
with a head full of dream
wondering about what her life
will one day be.

Somewhere in this world
there's a girl,
who one day wants to be
a star.
She can see herself standing
up on that bright stage,
her name in pink lights.

Somewhere in this world
there's a girl,
she still believes in
love at first sight.
She knows there's a person
who'll make her feel whole
and she knows that she'll find them
one day.

Somewhere in this world
there's a girl,
who doesn't know yet
how the world will destroy
all the belief and dreams
that kept her up at night
and that soon she'll be kept up
by sadness and dread
that can't be cured by lights.
She won't even believe in love,
let alone at first sight.

I dress like this

so that when I walk past a black, mirrored window I can catch a glimpse of myself and for a moment wonder who that beautiful woman is.

I dress like this so that I can look back at photos that my friend takes of me and not criticize every detail.

I dress like this so that the woman in Goodwill can talk excitedly about how well the orange of my cardigan matches the flowers on my pants.

I do not dress like this for you to talk at me out your window as I cross the street, and scream like animals as you drive away.

Civilized

Feed me to the wolves,
let me live among the bears,
I'll go swimming with the sharks,
take my chances in the jungle.
If the choice is between
the civilized or feral,
I'll always choose the animals
over the ferocity of men.

Get your shit together

"Is your refrigerator running? Because at this point, I'll vote for it." – goodluckkarly

Get your shit together,
good ol' America.
Land of the free,
home of violated trust.

Get your shit together,
you're a country built on corruption,
and prejudice,
and courts with too much power.

Get your shit together,
start protecting your people
and their rights
and their lives.

Get your shit together
before you go too far
and you end up looking like a
2010s YA dystopia novel.

Get your shit together.
Say it doesn't affect me?
But our border sometimes looks more
like a mirror than a line.

Get your shit together
before you have no more
people to vote for your
favourite old white guys.

Get your shit together
or else someone is going to decide
'enough is enough'
and put it together for you.

Birthday wishes

I wish for health for my family
and everyone else who needs it.
I wish for fair governments that
protect their peoples' rights.
I wish that every person be
allowed to live in peace.
I wish for the planet to stop fucking burning.
I wish that every child
see their next birthday.
I wish for a year where I never want to die.

But these wishes seem too big
for a measly nineteen candles,
so I guess for now I wish for
a year that's a little less shitty.

www.ingramcontent.com/pod-product-compliance
Lightning Source LLC
Chambersburg PA
CBHW030559080526
44585CB00012B/423